34TH CONGRESS, 3d Session. | SENATE. | Ex. Doc. No. 51.

REPORT

OF

THE SECRETARY OF WAR,

COMMUNICATING,

In compliance with a resolution of the Senate of the 5th instant, a copy of the report of Captain Thomas J. Cram, of November, 1856, on the oceanic routes to California.

FEBRUARY 16, 1857.—Read, ordered to lie on the table and be printed.

WAR DEPARTMENT,
Washington, February 13, 1857.

SIR: In compliance with the resolution of the Senate of the 5th instant, I have the honor to transmit herewith a copy of the "report from Captain Thomas J. Cram, of corps of topographical engineers, of November, A. D. 1856, on the oceanic routes to California."

Very respectfully, your obedient servant,

JEFF'N DAVIS,
Secretary of War.

Hon. J. M. MASON,
President pro tem. of the Senate.

Memoir on ocean routes between Atlantic and Pacific ports of the United States, extracted from Military Topographical Memoirs, by Captain T. Jefferson Cram, United States corps of Topographical Engineers, Chief Topographical Engineer Military Department of the Pacific, November, 1856.

PREFACE.

At the present time why do the means of transit across the narrow strip of land called Central America occupy, with so much intensity, the public mind of the people of the United States and Great Britain?

The sources of this anxiety are of a two-fold nature—political and commercial.

Of the former it is not my intention to speak, except incidentally; that is a subject better befitting the pens of Marcy and Clarendon;

but of the latter, I will here present a few facts by way of answering, in some degree, the leading question with which I have started.

To say nothing of what there will be in future at the present time, there are being passed over this isthmus 80,000 passengers, 81,000,000 dollars in treasure per annum, between the Pacific and Atlantic ports of the United States.

There is need of more rapidity of transmission of the public mails and treasure. The military service of the department of the Pacific requires more facilities, greater despatch, and cheaper rates of transportation. There is demanded better accommodations for all classes of passengers. To these may be added the demands of the Australia trade and travel, amounting to $44,000,000 in treasure, and 53,000 passengers, and imports from England alone of $73,000,000 per annum.

These are considerations in reference to this transit having an immediate connexion with the California and Australia trade. But there are others of equal moment, though not quite so near the vision, and therefore not so dazzling, viz: the general trade of the South American Pacific States, of the Pacific islands, and that of the centres of oriental commerce in India, China, and Japan, also having important demands on this transit.

What wonder, then, that the public mind, in this age of progress, is so much alive to the means of making it?

It should be no matter of surprise, therefore, that the enlightened "Chamber of Commerce of Liverpool" took up the subject recently, and resolved, by unanimous vote, to promote the immediate completion of the Hondurus interoceanic railway.

I quote from the remarks of Mr. Ewart, M. P., who said:

"The importance of the project could not be overrated. It is most desirable to improve the communication between the two oceans, and with the guaranty of England, France, and America, they could hardly doubt of success."

Mr. Brown, M. P., said:

"He thought it a fair subject for the Chamber of Commerce to take up with a view to the progressive commerce of the world. But independent of this view it had certain bearings upon the settlement of a question in which they were all interested—the much vexed question of Central America, involving, as it does, so many elements of discord between England and the United States."

The sea routes between the Atlantic and Pacific ports are becoming more and more multiplied according to the views of capitalists, the interests of commerce, the convenience, taste, safety, and means of the traveller or emigrant. And especially are these routes becoming varied by the modifications arising from the completion of railways on the Atlantic coast, so that at present there are four prominent routes—the Panama, the Nicaragua, the Honduras, the Tehuantepec—soon to be in active emulation, forcibly demonstrating the magnitude of the existing intercourse between the Pacific and Atlantic States. It is in reference to all these routes that I intend in this memoir to briefly speak, but more particularly of the last named, with a view to present some general considerations in reference to its importance among the great thoroughfares between our own Atlantic and Pacific ports; and this, too, without the slightest intention of disparagement to the advantages claimed in the meeting of the Liverpool Chamber of Commerce for the Honduras route beyond what may actually result from physical character. The advantages claimed in that meeting had a more particular application to the commerce of Europe than to that of the United States.

The accompanying charts are constructed upon the most accurate data attainable from the most recent observations in reference to latitudes and longitudes, hydrographic and other surveys, and will clearly exhibit to the eye the various routes, with all their modifications consequent upon railroads, stage roads,—whether of plank, stone, or gravel—now or soon to be constructed across the State of Florida, the island of Cuba, or Central America.

In recording distances, I use the *statute mile* instead of the nautical mile. Should a distance herein given be required in nautical miles, it will be at once obtained by multiplying the number of statute miles by the fraction 0.8675, and the product will be the number of nautical miles in that distance.

It is also to be understood that the rate per mile of the steamers' runs are also expressed, in this memoir, in statute miles; and, in speaking of a steamer's run, I have reference to the shortest practical route she can pursue between the two termini of her trip.

The subjects will be treated in the order of the routes, as already named, devoting one chapter to each.

I. PANAMA ROUTE.

It is well known that the journey from New York to San Francisco is effected on this, by a steamer leaving the former place semi-monthly, touching generally, though not necessarily, at Kingston, Jamaica, to coal and land a mail, &c.; thence to Aspinwall, following the route indicated by the dotted line, (chart No. 1;) crossing the isthmus by railway, 49 miles in length, between Aspinwall and Panama, and here embarking on a sea-steamer, which touches at Acapulco, Mexico, to coal, and thence directly to San Francisco, California, following the route in the Pacific dotted on chart No. 2.

For the transit across the isthmus 24 hours are generally consumed between the arrival of the Atlantic steamer, at Aspinwall dock, and departure of the corresponding Pacific steamer, from her mooring in Panama bay, with passengers, mail, and freight, all aboard for San Francisco. The mere time in the cars, however, is only 3 to 5 hours. At the Atlantic terminus the sea-steamer comes directly to the dock, in a good harbor, and the passengers have only to walk the plank to step, as it were, into the cars. But at the Pacific terminus it is different; here, on arriving at the railroad depot, which is near the water's edge, they are all immediately crowded on a steam-lighter boat, of shallow draft, and transported over the Panama bay, two or more miles, to the Pacific steamer—the shoalness of water not allowing steam ships a nearer approach to the shore.

The Panama Railroad Company deserve high praise for their superintendency of this transit. It is generally accomplished with sufficient despatch; nevertheless, the total time from New York to San Francisco is no shorter, if so short, as when the transit was made upon mule back, which sometimes required as many days as it now takes hours. This is no fault of the railroad company. The delay is attributable to the steamship companies, and is totally unjustifiable.

The Panama railroad will stand a noble monument of skill in structure, and of perseverance in overcoming natural difficulties in its progress, from its inception to the laying of the last rail. It is stamped with a world-renown as one of the most gigantic works of the age, and clothed with a national importance to the commercial nations.

The engineering on this work merits a passing notice, and important details could be stated in reference to it which would afford many valuable practical lessons of peculiar force, in the construction of any similar work in a tropical climate; but it would be out of place here to dwell on these particulars. Suffice it to say, the steepest grade is about 65 feet to the mile, and that only for a short distance. As fast as the first sleepers—which are of pine—decay, they are renewed with lignumvitæ sleepers. The short-span bridges are of iron superstructure, and when the wood of the two long-span bridges decays iron is to be substituted. The abutments, piers, and culverts are stone masonry, and such as should characterize all similar works, little for ornament, but everything necessary for substantiality. The rails are 60 pounds to the yard. Large portions of the earnings of the road are being wisely expended in reducing grades, lessening curvature, and ballasting the track with broken stone: and it is the intention to extend the Pacific terminus to deep water, to obviate the present great inconvenience and danger in the mode of embarkation. The cost of the work has not been less than $7,000,000, and it may be well doubted if, under all the extraordinary difficulties it encountered, it could have been built for less by any constructing engineer under control of a company so remote from the spot. Of the four routes, it is the Panama that involves the greatest extent of travel between New York and San Francisco, and the greatest vicissitudes in climate, requiring the passengers to go from 40° 40′ north latitude, to a southern climate, within 7° 13′ of the equator, and thence northerly to 37° 48′ north latitude, making an extensive excursion from cold to heat and from heat to cold in a short time. This, in addition to the liability of yellow fever, by any detention at Kingston, Aspinwall, or Panama, has produced the impression that it is not altogether a healthy route.

The horrible acts of violence, so revolting to humanity and too shocking to modesty to be written, which were committed upon the passengers by the native people at Panama last spring, can never be forgotten. Those atrocities—for which, however, the company's agents ought not to be blamed—are, nevertheless, sufficient to show that it is not a route safe from violence to the persons and effects of the hosts who cross at Panama. And hence, it has become necessary for our government to station a vessel-of-war at each terminus, and should necessity require it, England and France would, no doubt, promptly respond to a call for further protection of this transit. To maintain such protective force will entail a heavy tax upon the public treasury; and the want of confidence in the natives must materially affect the popularity of this route. Indemnification for the past only will not restore confidence; security for the future is demanded, and must be had at any cost.

The time and distance, at the present rates of steam locomotion on this route, will now be considered by introducing extracts of results, from my "Memoir on United States Mail Route Distances, Atlantic and Pacific," recently written.

Between New York and Aspinwall, as measured from the logs of the steamers averaging many trips, both ways running, it is 2,392 miles, and the average time of all the boats in the line is 10½ days. Between arrival at Aspinwall dock and departure from Panama bay, the average time of transit is one day, and distance 51 miles. Between Panama bay and San Francisco, touching only at Acapulco, the distance by the logs, taking a mean of many trips of all the steamers, both ways running, is 3,775 miles, and the average time is 13½ days. Hence the totals between New York and San Francisco are 6,218 miles, and 25 days. I have computed geodetically the shortest lines it is possible for a steamer to run in calm water, and find from New York, by east end of Cuba, to Aspinwall, 2,263 miles, which is less by 129 miles than the average of the runs given by the logs; and between Panama bay and San Francisco, touching at Acapulco, 3,731 miles, which is less by 45 miles than what results from the logs.

The nearness to an agreement between the computed shortest possible runs and the runs actually given in practice is interesting, and shows how near, in point of distance, the steamers have attained in their average runs to the theoretical minimum of extent on both oceans. We are also shown by this comparison, that the causes opposing the run on the shortest line have a much greater effect in the Atlantic than in the Pacific. For the practical results show that on the former a steamer, striving for the shortest run between two points, will make her total run longer by 0.054 of her count than the theoretical distance on a tranquil sea, whilst on the latter, it is only 0.012 of her total count. To make this plainer by an example, suppose that on the Atlantic she strives to make a run on the shortest run between two points, and finds her total count to be 100 miles; then will the shortest distance on a tranquil sea, between the same points, be only 94.6 miles, and on the Pacific, if her total run counts 100 miles, the shortest distance between the two points measured on a tranquil sea—suppose such a state possible—would be 98.8 miles.

Rates of speed of sea steamers.—It will be seen by the foregoing practical data, that the present average rate is, for the Atlantic between New York and Aspinwall, 9½ miles per hour, and on the Pacific, between Panama and San Francisco, it is 11⅔ per hour, including the time of one stoppage to coal on each ocean. The practical elements here given may be of service in projecting any new steamer line on either ocean to compete with those in operation. I am well aware that the ships from whose logs I have drawn my data *can* make greater speed, but the foregoing numbers are the actual measures of their working speed on these long trips. I am also well aware that the eminent builder, the late lamented Mr. Steers, guarantied, upon certain conditions, to construct steamers to run in the Atlantic proper at $20\frac{3}{4}$, and in the Gulf of Mexico, at 23 miles per hour, "and that the ships should not be surpassed in safety, comfort, and accommodation for passengers by any in the world;" and that there is a project on foot to establish lines in connexion with the Honduras transit, in which the ships shall come up to this speed.

Perhaps it would not be romancing to say, that in the Gulf, Atlantic, and on the Pacific, they ought to be made to perform at a mean between what they now do and the estimate of Mr. Steers, *i. e.*, on the Atlantic 15 miles and in the Gulf and Pacific $17\frac{1}{3}$ miles per hour, on long trips. But whether the demands of the interoceanic travel and trade can at present force them up to this work, is quite doubtful. Unless more rival lines are put in operation, it is not probable a higher speed will be attained than will best suit the convenience, economy, and profit of the companies, though they agree to convey the United States mail in ever so short a time. Connecting with the Panama line, there is the United States mail steamship line, from New Orleans to Havana, thence around the west end of Cuba to Aspinwall. The shortest run on which—from New Orleans to Havana— is 683 miles, and time two days, making the speed of the boat 14.23 miles per hour; and from Havana to Aspinwall the shortest run is 1,210 miles, and the time $5\frac{1}{4}$ days, averaging. This gives the working speed, in the Carribean sea, at the rate of 9.6 miles per hour.

The patronage of Congress has been very liberally bestowed, it must be acknowledged, upon the Panama route, in the way of immense sums paid for the transportation of mails and troops.

II. NICARAGUA ROUTE.

On this, the Atlantic steamers, on leaving New York, pursue about the same courses as on the Panama route, as far as to the east end of Cuba, whence they diverge towards the west, and pass between Cuba and Jamaica, thence directly for the mouth of the San Juan river, near which is Greytown.

On anchoring, small river steamers come along side and receive the passengers and baggage, and ascend the river to rapids, where a short portage is made to their head; here, all are again embarked in another set of river steamers, to ascend to other rapids, where another short portage is made. At the head of these, another embarkation takes place, upon other boats, to ascend to the outlet of Lake Nicaragua. At the outlet a transhipment occurs to a fine lake steamer, which runs to Virgin bay, where all are disembarked, and transported by wagons and mules over a good road, 12 miles, to San Juan del Sur, on the Pacific. Here the Pacific steamship receives the passengers, directly from a wharf boat, without the inconvenience of being rowed in small craft to the ship.

From San Juan del Sur, the course lies towards Point Angels, thence towards Pass Tejupan, thence into the port Manzanilla to coal, and land and receive passengers and specie; and for these purposes only, by permission of the Mexican government, is this line allowed to enter that port.

From this port the course lies to Point St. Lucas, thence the route is nearly the same to San Francisco as for the Panama line.

In navigating the San Juan river, at high stages, it is sometimes only necessary to make one portage around the rapids, and the short portages, not exceeding one mile, are made by walking. The length of the transit, from ocean to ocean, is 70 miles river navigation, 55 miles lake navigation, and 12 miles road travel, in all 137 miles. The time of making the transit has been quite variable, sometimes 3, at others 7 days, depending upon the stage of the river, winds on the lake, and whether it is being made up or down stream; as a general rule, the time is greater when going towards the Pacific than in an opposite direction. Taking the year through, a fair average both ways is probably about 4½ days. In order to attain the greatest speed on this transit, it would be necessary to construct a railroad. Lake Nicaragua is 128 feet above low tide of the Pacific, and 126½ above corresponding tide in the Atlantic. Between the lake and the Pacific there intervenes a summit 187 feet higher than the lake. About the year 1838, Mr. Bailey, of the British navy, made a survey of this transit, and the results are published in volume 1 of the late J. L. Stevens' Travels in Central America. The survey contemplated a canal, and made the distance from the Pacific to the summit 4 miles; from the summit to the lake, 11⅔ miles; and the length of the San Juan river, from the lake following the stream, 70 miles to the Atlantic.

I find, by a recent map of the lake, published by order of Congress, from data prepared at the United States Coast Survey Office, that the length of the west shore-line, starting from the point where Mr. Bailey's line ends at the lake, and going round to its outlet, which is the head of the San Juan river, is about eighty miles.

Let us now suppose the design of constructing a railroad from the Atlantic to the Pacific to accommodate the Nicaragua transit. By taking the foregoing data as a basis, we should have the first seventy miles with an average grade not exceeding eighteen feet per mile; and eighty miles along the lake shore, with an average grade of — feet per mile; and 11⅔ miles from the lake to the summit, at an average grade of sixteen feet per mile; and from the summit down to the Pacific, four miles, at an average grade of 77½ feet per mile; or, by increasing the length of this last section so as to make it five miles, we should bring the average grade down to 60.3 feet per mile.

So far, then, as the average grades go towards solving the problem, there would be no difficulty in the way of constructing a railroad along the route suggested, not exceeding 167 miles in length. As to the distribution of the grades in each section, however, no one can decide without more minute surveys than we have, and, consequently, though the practicability may be inferred, the degree of feasibility cannot be given. Should a railroad be constructed, the transit would be made in 8⅓ hours running time; and for the whole, from the arrival of the Atlantic sea steamer, the time would be only twenty-four hours before the corresponding Pacific steamer would be on her way.

The distances, times, and speed of the steamers on this route will now be considered for the journey from New York to San Francisco:

from New York to the mouth of San Juan river, the shortest run is 2,403 miles; length of transit 137 miles; run from San Juan del Sur to San Francisco, 2,964 miles. Total, 5,504 miles statute.

This makes the Nicaragua route shorter by 714 miles than the Panama route.

Now, although the former has this advantage in distance, still, owing to increased time for the transit, the average time for the whole journey has been found in practice to be about the same as on the Panama route, viz: twenty-five days.

The working speed of the steamers, taking both ocean runs, I find to be 10.67 miles per hour on the Nicaragua line, and 10.71 per hour on the Panama line.

The total southing on the Nicaragua is not so much by 2° 41′ as on the Panama route; and the variety, richness, and splendor of tropical scenery in the Nicaragua transit is not surpassed, if equalled, on any known route across the isthmus; in these respects, it has manifold advantages over the Panama transit. Owing, however, to the time requisite for making that transit, there is more danger of sickness on the former. Notwithstanding this drawback, the Nicaragua has been quite a popular route, especially in journeying eastward, and it has bravely vied with the Panama in spite of the whole patronage of the United States government in transportation of troops and mails, so lavishly bestowed on the latter.

The recent abrogation of the charter of the old company by General Walker's government in Nicaragua, and the granting of a new one to another company, and the revolutionary scenes so lately enacted, are circumstances tending to create an idea of much uncertainty and insecurity to passengers, and as a natural consequence, much less treasure is now being sent over this route than formerly. The line, however, is now, under the energy of the new company and the favor shown by General Walker, in regular operation once a month. And it is understood that elegant steamers are now being built, sufficient to re-establish the semi-monthly trips.

In connexion with this line there is one which merits consideration: between New Orleans and the mouth of the San Juan river, direct. The shortest run of the steamship is 1,430 miles; and the time of making the trip six days; working speed 9.93 miles per hour.

III. HONDURAS ROUTE.

For this, the most direct sea course would be from New York to Cape Hatteras; thence passing near Cape Florida; thence through the Gulf of Mexico, around by west end of Cuba; thence directly to port Caballo, on the Atlantic; thence across the Isthmus, through the state of Honduras, to the Gulf of Fonseca on the Pacific; thence to Acapulco; thence following the same course as the Panama, to San Francisco.

On this, the southing is not so much by about three degrees towards the equator as for the Nicaragua, and by five degrees and forty-five minutes as for the Panama route.

In reference to the transit across the isthmus of Honduras, I quote from the report of the proceedings of the Liverpool Chamber of Commerce already referred to :

"A charter for a railroad was obtained from the government of Honduras, April, 1855, providing the ports of both extremities, Porto Caballo and Fonseca, be free, and that all property in transitu be free of duty, and no passports be required of passengers. The state gives the company 1,500,000 acres of land, and concedes a bounty of seventy-five acres to each laborer in the employ of the company.

"The protection of both the United States and Great Britain is extended to this, in common with the other isthmus routes, by convention between these powers. The road is designed for freight and passengers, and to be 161 miles in length ; it is calculated to save not less than 1,300 miles sailing distance, over the Panama route, and to save seven to ten days in the voyages from Europe and the eastern ports of the United States, to the great centres of trade and travel in the Pacific, viz: California, the Sandwich Islands, Japan, and the East Indies. It is calculated by this route, at the present rate of speed, that passages can be made between New York and California in fourteen days ; from London or Paris to Australia, or China, in forty-five days. Other peculiar advantages are, that the railroad will pass through a country of eminent salubrity, and of vast mineral and agricultural wealth, ranking in these respects with the best part of Mexico, and unrivalled in respect of distance, cheapness of construction, climate, beauty of scenery, in local resources, and in perfectly safe harbors at its termini, accessible at all times by the deepest sea-going steamers and sail vessels. A population of 100,000 souls exists on the line which runs through Comayagua, the capital of Honduras."

Now, whether all that is here quoted will stand the test of analysis, according to the present rates of steam locomotion, will be seen by attention to the following facts :

Either the Honduras Company has made an error in reporting the length of their contemplated railroad, or there is a very considerable error in latitude or longitude of one or both of the termini, Porto Caballo or Fonseca ; I am not disposed to believe in the latter supposition. The shortest line—supposing a water level all the way from port to port—across the isthmus is 163½ miles. The actual length of the road to obtain suitable grades would, in all probability, be not less than 190 miles. But whether the road be a few miles longer or shorter is of little moment, viewed in reference to the magnitude of the undertaking. Let us suppose a good plank or railroad constructed, the running time in stages on the former would be 20 hours, and on the latter in cars 10 hours ; to which add 12 hours for disembarking and re-embarking, and we should have the time for the transit 32 hours, or 22 hours, according as the wooden or iron superstructure was used. The shortest run from New York to Porto Caballo would be 2,102 miles, requiring, according to the present working speed of the Atlantic steamers in the Panama line, 9½ days. The transit would consume one day. The shortest run from Fonseca to San Francisco would be 2,865 miles, requiring 10½ days, according to the present working rate of the Pacific steamers. And thus we see the total length of the journey, in miles, would be 5,157, and, in time, 21 days from

New York to San Francisco, instead of 14, as intimated in the report of the proceedings of the Chamber of Commerce. It is evident this route will be more direct than either the Panama or Nicaragua for almost all our Atlantic ports; for Porto Caballo can be reached by a sea run, or more direct and shorter sources, than can either Aspinwall or Greytown, as will be seen by the chart.

There is good reason for believing a railway across Honduras will be completed in a reasonable time, notwithstanding its cost, which, estimating from the cost of the Panama road, would not be short of $27,300,000—supposing it 190 miles long; but if we set it at only double the cost of the Baltimore and Susquehanna road, which was one of the most expensive in the United States, the Honduras railroad would cost, completed, nearly $24,000,000; but this is merely speculation; the cost can be estimated only upon accurate surveys. It is quite probable this transit will, ere long, be in readiness to convey passengers across in stages, and that the line will be in active operation between New York and San Francisco. And it is worthy of remark, that not only would the time be lessened by four to five days, but there would be less change of climate on this than on either route further south.

It is fair to conclude there is considerable stability in the government of Honduras, and, consequently, confidence will be inspired in reference to the safety of the transit.

Harbors.—The chart I have before me of the Fonseca shows it to be well land-locked from all except the southwest winds, and the soundings show ample depth in the channels for steamships to enter. In reference to the harbors at the termini of this contemplated transit road, I will here quote from Mr. Totten, chief engineer of the Panama road. In a published letter, September 3, 1856, he says: "I see but one favorable feature in that [Honduras] route, which is the bay of Fonseca, on the Pacific, towards which Mr. Squiers seems to have an enthusiastic partiality. The proposed harbor terminus (Isabel) on the Atlantic side is only approachable by vessels of very light draft."

It seems that Lieut. Jeffers, United States navy, made a survey of Porto Caballo in 1854. Mr. Squiers concludes from the chart of this survey, "that in ease of entrance, depth of water, safety of anchorage, and all other essentials, this is the best port on the Atlantic coast of Central America, without exception;" and also strengthens his opinion of its advantages from the fact that Cortez regarded it as "the best port in all New Spain," in his letter to the Emperor Charles V.

Mr. Squiers is of the opinion Mr. Totten has altogether mistaken the Atlantic terminus of the proposed Honduras railroad, and so it would seem from the latter having assumed Isabel for the terminus.

IV.—TEHUANTEPEC ROUTE.

On this, the most direct sea run from New York is to follow the course to Cape Hatteras, thence by the Florida reefs, thence near Sisal, thence directly to the mouth of the Coatzacoalcos river. (See chart No. 1.) The route over the isthmus is from the mouth of the Coatzacoalcos, up its valley, across a dividing ridge; thence near by the town of Tehuantepec to Port Ventosa, on the Pacific. From this port, by sea-steamers, touching, if need be, at Acapulco to coal, thence following the same route the Panama line pursues to San Francisco, or, indeed, to all the ports above Acapulco.

It is evident, from a mere glance at the charts, the Tehuantepec route possesses peculiar advantages over the other routes, especially in regard to the commerce of the ports of the United States, both Atlantic and Pacific. For although the runs in the Atlantic, from New York and the ports south until we get to Cedar Key, would be a little shorter to the terminus of the Honduras transit, still for all our ports further south than Cedar Key, the runs would be shorter to the terminus of the Tehuantepec transit. And all our ports on the Pacific are much nearer the Tehuantepec than either of the other transits.

Besides, the runs from all our ports, north of Cape Florida, would be brought more and more within the less boisterous waters of the Gulf of Mexico, and from all south of that cape they would be entirely within the gulf, and a more genial climate would be realized, the total southing towards the equator not being so much by three degrees as for the Honduras route.

I think it clearly established, that in points of distance, shortness of sea voyage, vicissitudes of climate, tranquillity of waters, and speed, the Tehuantepec route for the commerce and travel between the United States ports has decided advantages over all others.

Mr. Webster, in a speech in the Senate, expressed it as his decided opinion, after mature examination of the subject, "that our government should omit no proper efforts to induce the Mexican government to co-operate in the opening of this transit, as it was destined to be all-important to the interests of the people of both republics." I have claimed decided advantages for the whole route; but in reference to merely making the isthmus transit it may be otherwise. In order to judge of this question, I will briefly state what has been proposed, and what is being done to make it a suitable transit for passengers and treasure.

Had not the Mexican government stopped the work, first openly evincing its opposition by ordering a military force to the isthmus in 1851 to enforce the decree to expel the surveying party from the country, this route would, probably, at the present time have been in successful operation. A cordial co-operation, not only on the part of the Mexican government, but likewise of rival companies, claiming the right to construct the road, is necessary to success.

It is only since President Comonfort came into power that a more enlightened policy has obtained, so that now there is a belief the work of improving this transit is going rapidly onward, under the influence of picks, spades, drills, and carts. * * *

It seems the immediate undertaking consists in making a wagon road from the head of river navigation, on the Coalzacoalcos, to Port Ventosa, 118 miles in length. From the Atlantic to this head of river navigation, it is also 118 miles by the river, which is navigable at lowest stage for steamers drawing two feet, as shown by the soundings of Lieutenant Temple, United States navy, who made the survey in 1851. It is believed the greatest difficulties in the way of making an excellent wagon road have already been overcome; and in no place have they proved at all formidable. On the 3d of October last it was published in the Mexican papers, "that fifty-three miles of the road were ready for carriages; that the place where the heaviest earth and rock excavations existed had 110 men employed on it; that two thirds of the whole extent had been grubbed and cleared; and that the company had ample means and no lack of energy to continue the work," &c. Now, this certainly looks like determined purpose, and this carriage road may be regarded as the first efficient work towards opening the Tehuantepec transit.

A good stage road across this isthmus is the necessary forerunner of a rail way surely to follow.

We hail the prediction of Webster as beginning to be fulfilled under American enterprise. Let the stage road be put in operation, and steamers be placed on both oceans, to run in connexion, and there can be no doubt in the mind of one who will examine the subject in its multifarious bearings, that this will immediately become the most popular route, and there wants no rail road speed in the transit to make it sought by a very large portion of the travelling throngs that pass between our Atlantic and Pacific ports. The direct distance from the mouth of the Coatzacoalcos to Ventose is 140 miles; but by the river and carriage road, now being constructed, it is, as we have seen, 236 miles. This road may be made to become a great stage thoroughfare, great in proportion to the excellence of accommodation and speed of the steamers connected with it. "The country rises gradually from the coast of each ocean, and from the route being in the line of direction of the trade winds, it is remarkably healthy, and no malignant fevers exist on it, and the thermometer rarely rises above 80 to 85 degrees, and the scenery all along is magnificent."

Distances and Times.—From New York to the mouth of the Coatzacoalcos the shortest run is 2,275 miles, and the time, according to the present rates of speed in the Atlantic and Gulf, would be 9¾ days. The transit, 236 miles from ocean steamer to ocean steamer, would require 2¾ days, supposing only 4 miles per hour on the wagon road and 6 miles per hour on the river, and allowing 18 hours for transhipments and stoppages. From Ventosa to San Francisco the shortest run is 2,304 miles, which, at the present rate of speed in the Pacific, would require 8¼ days. These give the totals between New York and San Francisco 4,815 miles, and time 20¾ days.

Thus it seems this route is shorter than the Panama by 1,403 miles, and 4¼ days in time; and less than the Honduras by 342 miles, and by ¼ day in time, notwithstanding the railroad at Panama; and though there should be one for the Honduras, and only the river and a wagon road for this, the Tehuantepec route.

Should the Tehuantepec Company, however, put their design in execution, of constructing a substantial railroad from Minititlan to Ventosa, 166 miles in length, on which in no place would the maximum grade exceed 60 feet per mile, then would the transit be made in 20 hours from ocean steamer to ocean steamer, and the Tehuantepec route between New York and San Francisco would have the advantage of a saving of $6\frac{1}{4}$ days over the Panama, and of $2\frac{1}{4}$ days over the Honduras.

This, be it observed, supposes a railroad in operation on each transit.

If we adopt a mean between that proposed by Mr. Steers and the present working speed, we should, supposing a railroad, have the total time on the Tehuantepec route from New York to San Francisco, only 12 days 4 hours. This would put the ships up to 15 miles per hour on the Atlantic, and $17\frac{1}{3}$ miles in the Gulf and the Pacific, and allow *one* day for the transit.

In comparing the Tehuantepec with the Honduras, or other routes, the considerations of the costs of the respective railroads, or of which may have the best harbors at the termini of the transits, are undoubtedly of moment; but they are by no means the paramount considerations. The greater elements—time, shortness of sea voyage, comfort, and safety—will establish the supremacy of the route. To enter into all the particulars in reference to the feasibility of the contemplated railroad would extend this memoir unreasonably. To those, however, who wish for proof entire of the degree of feasibility, I would recommend a reference to that masterly report on "The Isthmus of Tehuantepec," by J. J. Williams, esq., civil engineer, principal assistant engineer, endorsed by Major Barnard, chief engineer, published in 1852.

That report embraces every circumstance bearing on the subject, and contains valuable contributions to science from a gifted mind; its contents deserve a more widely extended circulation in a popular form to reach the minds of the people of Mexico and of the United States, who are most deeply interested in this route, than can be well realized from a single expensive volume.

But, however averse to entering on details, there are some that ought not in justice to be here omitted, and these pertain to the natural facilities of the harbors at the termini of the Tehuantepec transit. For the Atlantic terminus, the harbor is the lower part of the Coatzacoalcos river, from its mouth up to Minititlan, for an extent of twenty miles. In relation to the bar at the mouth of this river I refer to the survey of Commander Lynch, United States navy, in 1848, as published in a chart from the United States Hydrographical Office, which gives the depth on the bar $12\frac{1}{2}$ feet shoalest place at lowest tides. I also refer to an examination by Captain Foster, of the steamship Alabama, who crossed the bar several times, and has given directions for entering the river under the worst winds that occur. He reports:

"The bar, by actual measurement, to be [from deep water on the inner to corresponding depth on the outer side] only 108 feet in breadth; the bottom, composed of sand and clay, is hard, and on this account does not shift; the general depth on the bar is not less than twelve feet, from which the water deepens gradually to nearly thirty feet each way."

From the bar the Coatzacoalcos river carries a width of one fourth to one third of a mile, and a depth of eighteen feet, at least for twenty miles above, up to Minatitlan, and of sixteen feet for ten miles higher up, at lowest stages; as shown by the soundings of Lieutenant Alden, United States navy, in 1847.

It is proven, beyond doubt, that the character of the bottom is such that no material shifting of the channel or change in the bar has occurred since it was first known to the Spanish navigators; and a sufficient evidence of permanency is furnished by the simple fact, that, from that time to the present day, this river has continued to debouch, in a due north direction, into the very bottom of the Gulf of Mexico, in spite of the northers that sweep in an opposite direction. In consequence of this permanency, improvements by deepening the channel on the bar would be likely to succeed; but there is, at present, no necessity for any improvement of the kind. Sea steamers constructed suitably for it, can now enter without difficulty when the channel is once properly marked by buoys, with a draft ample for safety in the navigation of the Atlantic anywhere on this route.

In reference to the harbor at the Pacific terminus, this is so much misunderstood and so differently reported by those who have never had an opportunity of personal observation or of an inspection of the chart, that I will not attempt to make statements without likewise giving authority to sustain me.

Ventosa, which is the Pacific terminus, is often confounded with Bocca Bara—the entrance from sea into lakes, twenty-five miles east of Point Morro. This point juts well out into the ocean, and covers from the north and west winds a capacious indentation, which is only exposed to the south and southeast winds. It is this bay that is the proper La Ventosa, having excellent anchorage and deep water near in-shore, no rocks, no islands or shoals in the offing to make it dangerous to enter at any time, however foggy. And in it, for a long extent, the water is ten feet deep within one hundred feet from the shore. By docking out 250 feet a little to the eastward of Point Morro, we get sixteen to eighteen feet water, deep enough for the largest class of sea steamers to lie alongside.

P. Trastour, esq., civil engineer, and Lieutenant Temple, United States navy, both propose an expensive breakwater to cover this harbor from the southeast, but do not agree upon the location; and this recommendation, I find, has been the foundation for the opinion of those who carelessly examine subjects, that a breakwater is indispensable at Ventosa. Nothing is more erroneous. The breakwater was only recommended as a desirable improvement *in futuro*, in reference to forming a capacious basin, which, if completed, would make La Ventosa an unexceptionable harbor for all kinds and classes of ships.

La Ventosa now, in its natural condition, presents a safe and commodious harbor to vessels of all sizes. Locked on the west by Morro heights and on the north by land, it is only open to the south and east, and it allows ingress and egress, irrespective of the quarter whence the wind blows. The depth at 350 feet from the shore generally is seventeen feet. The bed of the sea recedes with a regular grade of two feet increase of depth per 100 feet, horizontal; and the greatest observed distance between low and high water levels is six and a half feet. There is little doubt of the Bay La Ventosa affording a safer harbor than Vera Cruz, Mexico.

Captain Mott, master of the steamship Gold Hunter, (now the "Active,") says: "I am much pleased with this port, Ventosa. The holding ground is excellent, and the depth of thirty-six to forty-two feet all over the bay very convenient. I see nothing but a break-water carried out five hundred to six hundred yards from the outer point of Morro rock to protect the landing from the surf, to make it an excellent port. During the four days we have been here we have had two of fresh southerly winds, and two of strong northers; the former did not agitate the sea much, and the latter, though blowing very strong, has not straightened out our chains—we are still riding by the bight, which is buried in clay bottom."

Lieut. Temple, United States navy, says: "I am of the opinion La Ventosa is far safer and better than either Valparaiso, in Chili, or Monterey, in California—ports in constant use the whole year round. I speak from personal observation as well as from an examination of the several charts; and their similarity in outline has suggested the comparison," &c.

Under any circumstances affecting the question, it is clearly demonstrable that La Ventosa, at comparatively small expense, can be furnished with every facility for steamships to receive and discharge, by a simple dock 250 feet long; and we know it may be used without any artificial construction whatever, to better advantage for embarking and landing passengers and freight than is the bay of Panama; for, at the latter place, lighterage has to be used for an extent of two miles at least; whilst, at the former, if lighterage had to be used, it would only be for an extent not to exceed 300 feet.

On the bar at the mouth of the Tehuantepec river, which enters Ventosa bay a short distance east of Point Morro, I observe the chart gives four to five feet depth of water. This would admit of light draught steamboats for lighterage purposes at this terminus, which would have the advantage, when once over the bar and into the river, of still water for discharging and receiving.

V. MODIFICATIONS OF THE ROUTES BY A CONNEXION WITH THE CUBA AND FLORIDA RAILROADS.

In all that precedes, each inter-oceanic route has been considered as involving the condition of a continuous sea-run from the Atlantic ports to the termini of the isthmus transits. Now, a continuity of sea voyage is by no means a necessary condition, appertaining to the Atlantic portion of the routes; and it is well worth while to consider if any modifications may reasonably be expected in these routes by railroads, other than those across Central America; and if there be any to indicate the character and measure of the modification.

1. *Railway across the island of Cuba.*—This road is in operation entirely across from Havana to Batavano on the south side, where there is reported to be a favorable harbor for sea steamers. Havana being an important centre for commercial operations, and of travel for the West India islands and the Central American ports, all the

way south from Vera Cruz to Aspinwall, the Cuba railroad becomes a central link of land transit, and may be supposed capable of modifying, more or less, the great routes between our Atlantic and Pacific ports.

But this railway, if brought into connexion, can have no other effect on the question than that which may already be experienced in reference to the Panama route, viz: to enable travellers from the Gulf ports to more readily reach the Atlantic termini of the Panama, Nicaragua, and Honduras routes; and this supposes direct steamer lines between these termini and Batavano, a supposition not to be fully realized at present. Sooner than three such lines, we may expect to see *one* starting from Batavano, to run to Porto Caballo, thence coasting to Greytown and Aspinwall, thence returning directly to Batavano. The Cuba road, lying in a direct line between Cedar Key and Aspinwall, may become an important link in an express line, by alternate water and land from Aspinwall, across Florida, to New York. But whatever offices it may be expected to perform, there is one it cannot effect—it can never interfere, or have any connexion with, the Tehuantepec route.

2. *Florida railroad.*—The realization of this much and deservedly talked of road must now be regarded as a fixed fact, and as one of the most striking features in the systems of internal improvement of the States, so forcibly characterizing the age.

That this road will be in successful operation across the entire neck of the peninsula within a short time cannot be doubted by any one with but half an eye to present progress. It has not only the means—and that, too, in abundance—of the very best kind assigned by the Congress of the United States, on which funds are raised as they are needed, but it is now under contract, and being made for an extent of 137½ miles between Fernandina and Cedar key.

From the very able report, by the president of the company to the stockholders, in 1855, I learn that "the grades in no place exceed fifteen feet per mile, and the track is on an air line, and is to be laid with heavy rail."

This is wise; and the superstructure, once ballasted with broken stone, which can easily be done, the road will have the capacity of immense speed, and an express passenger train could make the whole distance in two hours seventeen and a half minutes in safety.

That the great land fund assigned by Congress for railroad purposes in Florida, under wise management will yield ample means to cover the cost of the works contemplated in the grant, should not be doubted; and under the impetus that will be given by the opening of this *principal* road, Florida may reasonably hope for the full fruition of a general system of roads, tending as much to promote her prosperity as such are known to have advanced the general welfare of other States.

From the time of the descent upon Florida by Hernando de Soto's band of Spaniards, in 1539, to the present day, the possession of the soil has probably caused more expenditure of blood in wars, of money to carry them on, and to purchase title, than any other portion of the globe. The strife between colonies for its possession, was stamped with sanguinary fierceness; and the tenacity with which this fair peninsula has been held by its aboriginal occupants has been truly wonderful, and scarcely equalled in strength by the exerted power of the people of two civilized nations to wrest it from the savage hand; for it is yet the scene, in some parts, of a war strife for possession.

May not all this cost of life and money be sufficient evidence of the immensity of the value of Florida? If not, then let Florida speak for herself, by her geographical position, salubrity of climate, fertility of soil—it being the only portion of the United States where tropical staples of all kinds can be successfully raised—by her military and commercial position, her harbors, adaptation for easy transit by railroads and artificial canals and naturally navigable rivers, and by her forest and other products, which are peculiar to her soil and climate. The truth is, Florida possesses the natural elements of greatness in an eminent degree; to deny it, would be tantamount to ignoring all those resources which she is known to possess, and which are necessary to constitute a first class State in the republic.

It would be out of place here to enter into details; those, however, who desire particulars, may refer to the able and very interesting series of letters (six in number) on the "Climate, Soils, and Productions of Florida," by Surgeon Byrne, United States army, embodying results of his own observations, published in 1843, in the National Intelligencer. His opportunities for observation, during seven years' service in that field, were undoubtedly greater than those enjoyed by any other person, and that his letters do justice to the peninsula none can doubt.

But, however bountiful soever nature may be in the bestowal of her gifts upon a State, it is appointed for man to be the agent for their development into a condition of practical utility to the common weal. On reviewing the past history of works of internal improvement in our country, it is plainly discernible that the first, or leading work, executed in a State, has been sure to mark the era of her highest prosperity. To this general rule the Florida railroad will prove no exception; and for that genius shown in the inception, that practical judgment so necessary for organizing means to the end, that energy of purpose, so essential to execution, evinced in connexion with this leading or principal work, Florida will stand as much indebted to her Yulee as New York to her Clinton, for the like qualities and services bestowed on that State.

It is time, however, to return to the object of this memoir, viz: to discuss the connexion of the Florida railroad with the commercial routes of interoceanic travel. It is seen on the chart that this railroad intervenes in continuation of the direct route between New York and the Tehuantepec transit, and also conveniently in the Honduras route, and it also intervenes directly between our Gulf ports and all our middle and northern ports. The vast trade between which may be expressed in figures, as follows: In 1852, the Treasury Department estimated it at $325,000,000 per annum. In the excellent report of Lieutenant M. L. Smith, (now captain,) corps of topographical engineers, on the "United States survey for a ship canal across the peninsula of Florida," the trade is estimated, in 1855, at $450,000,000—giving an annual increase of $42,000,000. In connexion with such a trade, the Florida railroad cannot fail to become of great moment, especially as it will shorten the distance so much between the principal ports carrying it on.

Thus, the shortest sea-steamer run from New York to Fernandina is 909 miles; thence by railroad to Cedar Key, 137½ miles; thence the shortest sea-steamer run to New Orleans is 467 miles. Total between New York and New Orleans, 1,513 miles, while the continuous sea run around Cape Florida is 1,872 miles—giving 359 miles saving by using this railroad.

But whether this railroad will be likely to enter into connexion, so far as to form a permanent link with the Honduras and Tehuantepec routes, will materially depend upon harbor facilities at its extremities for first-class sea-steamers.

Experienced assistants of the United States Coast Survey, appointed to examine Cedar Key harbor, report: "It is easy of access, holding ground good, has an anchorage of about one mile in extent, the deep water of which is readily reached by piers, and that ten feet at low, and fully twelve feet at ordinary high water can be carried into it. The general depth in the harbor is fourteen feet."

The Fernandina harbor was known during the Spanish possession as one of the best southern harbors. It still retains that character, as shown by a recent survey by an officer of the United States corps of topographical engineers. The chief of the corps of engineers, General Totten, reports it, after examining that survey, "as one of the safest and most accessible. This is the most southern port accessible to vessels of war, and is nearest the great channel of trade flowing through the Florida Straits The depth is fourteen feet on the bar at low, and twenty feet at ordinary high, and twenty-three feet at spring tides."

From my own experience, in connexion with the harbors of the Gulf, those on the northern lakes, and on the Atlantic and Pacific, in reference to their adaptation for steamships, and from the foregoing data, in reference to Cedar Key, I have no hesitation in assuring ship-builders that steamers of suitable draft, of excellent accommodation for passengers, swiftness, and safety, can be easily built to ply most successfully in the Gulf, directly between Cedar Key and the Atlantic terminus of the Tehuantepec transit. But to bring all the Atlantic steamers, now employed on the interoceanic routes, into connexion with the Cedar Key harbor would require a system of lighterage that at present would not be profitable.

In relation to the Fernandina harbor, it is scarcely necessary to say it affords a capital terminus for any new sea-steamer line, whether to Europe, or to either of the termini of the isthmus transits, or to any of our ports north of it, in so far as harbor facilities are required. Under all considerations, especially those demanding the utmost speed in the transportation of mails, troops, and travellers, so probable is it the Florida railroad will yet form a second land transit on the Tehuantepec route, that I will give the saving of time that may be effected by it for the journey between New York and San Francisco—a journey that will still be a long one, however much it may be shortened by human skill and commercial rivalry.

"*Tehuantepec-Florida route.*"—Taking for data the present working rates of speed of the steamers now running between New York and Savannah, between New York and Havana and in the Gulf, between New Orleans and Havana, and of the Pacific steamships, and making an appropriate application of these working speeds, the distances and times become as follows:

Between New York and Fernandina the average sea-steamer run of many trips, both ways, would be 909 miles; requiring two days and seventeen hours.

Transit by the Florida railroad, 137½ miles, at 30 miles per hour, and allowing twelve hours for disembarking, re-embarking, and stoppages, would require sixteen and a half hours.

Between Cedar Key and the mouth of the Coatzacoalcos river the average sea-steamer run would be 1,047 miles, and the time three days and one and a half hour.

The Tehuantepec transit, 236 miles by river and stage road—6 miles per hour on the former and 4 on the latter—and allowing eighteen hours for disembarking, stoppages, and re-embarking, would require two days and eighteen hours.

Between Ventosa and San Francisco the average sea-steamer run—stopping once to coal—is 2,304 miles; and the time would be eight days and six hours.

Total distance between New York and San Francisco, 4,633 miles; and the time seventeen days and eleven hours. Hence, by using the Florida railroad in the Tehuantepec line, we should save 182 miles of that extremely dangerous navigation around Cape Florida, and save three days and seven hours in time.

These results, it must be remembered, suppose no railroad over the Tehuantepec isthmus; nor do they involve a higher rate of speed than the present practical working of the sea-going vessels propelled by steam power.

Now, let us suppose the Tehuantepec railroad in operation, and the steamers put up to the speed of a mean between what Mr. Steers proposed and what they now perform; also, an express speed on the Florida railroad, (because with it there would be competition,) but only an ordinary speed on the Tehuantepec railroad, and the times would be:

	Days.	Hours.
From New York to Fernandina....................................	2	4
Florida transit, (from ocean steamer to ocean steamer)......		14½
From Cedar Key to Coatzacoalcas................................	2	8
Tehuantepec transit, (from steamer to steamer)................		20
From Ventosa to San Francisco..................................	5	4
Total, from New York to San Francisco......................	11	2½

By not using the Florida railroad, but in all other respects making the same supposition as above, the total time between New York and San Francisco would be twelve days and four hours.

We thus perceive there would be an average advantage of the saving of one day and two hours by using the Florida railroad. And a corresponding result would be found supposing any speed that steamships can be made to attain under any circumstances of competition.

It is, therefore, clearly proven that by the "Tehuantepec-Florida route," in making the journey between New York and San Francisco, we avoid the dangerous navigation around Cape Florida; we have more variety; we have less sea voyage, and we gain time, besides; and that this will be the shortest, most healthy, and less dangerous route between our Pacific ports and all those on the Atlantic north of Cedar Key; and that we may reasonably look forward to the time when the journey between New York and San Francisco will be accomplished by the traveller, and a regiment of troops transported, in eleven days and two and a half hours, instead of twenty-five days, as at present.

Respectfully submitted.

Col. J. J. Abert,
Chief of the Corps Topographical Engineers.

www.ingramcontent.com/pod-product-compliance
Lightning Source LLC
LaVergne TN
LVHW020636110826
845149LV00004B/1218
* 9 7 8 1 4 1 8 1 9 1 2 7 6 *